near death (domestic)

poetry

maggie sullivan

tall-lighthouse

for my mum

Thanks to dad, Irene, Leila Rendel, James King,
Peter Sullivan, Robert, Louise, Peter Carpenter,
Michael Donaghy, Ann, Phil, Sound Crew
and Jan Pontifex, for their extraordinary guidance.

Poems, or versions of poems in this book, have appeared
in Smiths Knoll, RIALTO, Obsessed with Pipework,
Nth Postion, Poets Letter, automatic lighthouse, ORBIS.
and Room (an anthology of poetry from the Tonbridge
Poetry Competition 2006)

Epigraph is taken from the poem *Broken Love Waltz*
by Aoife Mannix published in the tall-lighthouse
poetry anthology *automatic lighthouse*

cover image: mat redvers

© Maggie Sullivan 2007
Maggie Sullivan has asserted her right under
the Copyright, Design and Patents Act 1988
to be identified as the author of this work.

ISBN 978-1-904551-34-8
tall-lighthouse
www.tall-lighthouse.co.uk

contents

Scene Set	1
Frame	2
The Hitch	3
The Weather on Our Street	4
No Bag	5
Meanwhile, back indoors	6
Sherbert Lemons	7
An Everyday Epic	8
Lot's Wife	9
House Rules	10
Addition	11
Late Flowering	12
Plumb Line	13
Jigsaw	14
The Man in a Skin Suit	15
A Rough Sleeper Works Out	16
Remains on a Helpline	17
Xpressions	18
Break	19
Finishing Line	20
Cleavage	21
Dimensions	22
Inheritance	23
Near Death (Domestic)	24
Windolene	25
Lexicon	26
Suspending Belief	
i *Pink Elephant*	27
ii *Feather House*	28
iii *South to North*	29
iv *Dancing*	30
Love and the Law of My Children	31
My Most Faithful Audience	32
Touching the Grain	33
Soundings	34
Funny Bones	35
Final Soundtrack	36
RSVP	37

All the beautiful poetry in the world
can't turn a heart around when it's
bent on suicide
                        Aoife Mannix

Scene Set

Welcome,
imprinted on the door mat
like a smile.

Act One,
cue feet.

Frame

Square cut fringe,
a button up blouse,
grey pleated skirt,
an exercise book, open
and a pen.

Now, smile for the camera.

A regular school photograph -
but not quite. One student
sits at right angles,
tight lipped,

the close up
and long shot.

The Hitch

Nobody knew of a just
cause or impediment.

The bride and groom repeated
after the vicar without tripping
over their vows.

In the congregation
much clearing of throats
and the rustle of hats

as the vicar leads the newlyweds
off to sign the register
and while the ink dries
the confetti flows.

Later, in the dark room
the photographer lifts the first
of the proofs, very carefully.

The Weather on Our Street

A hurricane jumped the fence,
blew in through the door
we'd forgotten to lock,
found the soul of the most fragile,
worked up a storm
at the heart of the house,

one dead
three of us beached with the debris;
not a chair left unbroken
and only half a pot of glue
to re-shape a future.

You'd know our house now for its hoard
of sticking plaster and umbrellas,
still trying to hold the corner.

No Bag

The house hoovered, I thought
why stop at these four walls,
the street could do with a good clean.

Merritt Road pristine I paused
at the junction, realized I'd found
an extended modus operandi

but needed a bigger machine
so I took a sabbatical in the garage,
adapted the Dyson.

Wow, the improved model
straddled both lanes.
Added features –
unlimited tonnage,
heat seeking.
Night vision found muck in all manner
of corners. Its dual action telescopic nozzle
got under the whitewash and up
every stubborn nose,
locked on.

Smell rising.
Now, I said,
*either you take a good long sniff
or this appliance will sneeze.*

Meanwhile, back indoors

Through the window, she nods
to Mr Johnson walking his dog,
new couple at number three,
milk float passing,
her single pint no consolation.
Somebody skimmed the cream
off her pension.

Wait for the post, just in case,
a little shopping -
there is always the free bus pass,

and so few buses
through the new estate.
Nurse due at two
who always asks
How are we today?

She could better demonstrate
her answer with a semi-automatic
but the nurse is satisfied,
will see her *Next week as usual.*

At five,
she adds gun
to the shopping list.
There's a bit left in the bank.

Sherbert Lemons

A reward
for being good
and doing what she's told.

Mum says she must always
tell the truth, but dad
wants it kept a secret.

An Everyday Epic

A toddler,
a baby,
four bags of shopping,
a hill,
then a wheel falls off the pram.

The children are in conspiracy today –
it's a nappy marathon
but the washing machine
is still in the repair shop.

She is in the garden
burying shopping, pram wheel,
nappies and washing machine
as deep

as she can,
tucks the children up in their beds.
They sense her mulch of rage and tenderness.

Lot's Wife

I don't look back,
too busy making a pound of mince stretch
or explaining the purpose of the shower curtain.

Each day I tend to the rendering, point out
keys, wallet, PE kit, lunchbox
ranged round like commandments.
I keep them, watch over fridge and wardrobe
but the endless supply of clean, ironed shirts
are commonplace miracles,
go unacknowledged.

It's a long walk away from Sodom and Gomorrah
with little reward. Mine
the cornflakes left at the bottom of the box
and plastic toy
like a small memorial cruet –

not even a life size pillar of salt.

House Rules

You entered and the house reacted
like an insecure child. That tap
I thought I'd fixed resumed its drip, drip, drip
of interrogation. Ghosts in the cellar whispered
Is he safe? Can he be trusted?

This need to know, in advance
the exact duration of your visit,
all the intentions. The old broom beating
its tattoo, *What is love? What is love?*
What is love, precisely?
Pots and pans in constant dispute
with the dishwasher.
The calendar always assumes an end date.

Never say *You'll find out*,
that's death to the rug,
no gaps in my cupboards
though I like the way you open them, handle
an oil can, approach the fridge
unafraid

and you have won over the duvet;
it has warmed to the way you slip your hand
under my left breast each night,
bring it to rest over my heart, as if to say
You can break now.

Addition

When he arrived with roses
and again the next week
and the week after that
I forgot to count beyond three.

Now, alone with an empty vase
and an abacus strung with petals
the sum is irrefutable –

I never asked for flowers.

Late Flowering

Her husband's home
bearing fists full of flowers,
black daffodils, a bloom of bruises
she hides from the kids, neighbours.
He likes this private arrangement.

She would prefer a more open viewing
but he's built the walls too high for her to climb,
locks the garden with a perennial sense
                              of grievance.
She tries to repair the soil.
He stalks the beds, stakes the buds
as far from the gate as possible,

admits no brokerage.
Tomorrow, the coroner will record
another case of black daffodils.
Her husband will be inconsolable.

Plumb Line

First box of bricks,
all those wobbly towers,
getting the hang of how they stand

then that fight with the kid next door
over who could build highest.
Blood got into the cement.

Older, out with a hard hat
and a blueprint for a monolith,
tallest landmark on the sky line.
It blocks your neighbour's view –

old scores to settle.
Much more blood in the rubble.

Jigsaw

There isn't a finished picture on the lid.
You must climb into the box, subterranean,
skewed. Breathe the wrecked atmosphere,

search for the pieces
with arc light and lifting gear,
un-weld limbs from metal,
work out which leg goes with which torso.
There is a foot left over.

No recognisable corners
or straight edges.
This foot doesn't fit anyone

and there is never enough sky.

The Man in a Skin Suit

He sits naked and motionless
on a box set down in a doorway,
looks for all the world
like a latter day Adam
sent to test the rumour
that an Eden existed here once.

A hard landing,
he struggles to get his bearings -
air heavy and not so clean as before,
more concrete than green.
A disbelieving crowd gathers.
He lifts a finger, points
at the shoppers and tourists

and even if our grounding asserts
he's really a street artist
in a cleverly crafted skin suit,
he does it so well,
we all hold our breath,

watch as he unfolds on the pavement,
signs the distance travelled.

A Rough Sleeper Works Out

You need to be fit
to live on the street
but, cash-strapped
for a subscription
to a fancy gym,
learn to improvise:

rocks for weights,
big bits of rubble.
He works out with them
stripped to the waist
on the concourse
at Charing Cross Station,
lifts each arm in turn,
muscles strain to extend their reach
while the commuters give him
a wider berth than usual
and the police call up reinforcements.

I don't think he'll move on quietly this time -
eyes heavy with anger,
again and again he lifts those rocks
until he's got them high enough to hurl
at the rest of us
like so much small change.

Remains on a Helpline

Phones still clamped to ears when we expired.
This will be a mark of modern man
for archaeologists,
coffins reshaped to accommodate
the fixed v of elbow,
as cramp took hold,
blood stopped flowing
and gangrene set in.

But note, also, that Jerusalem
is still playing faintly, punctuated
by the soporific tone of the recorded message
attempting to placate our remains.

They'll dig us up years from now,
put our relics on show
in the gallery of twenty first century curiosities.
Call this era

Rigor mortis, with handpiece and soundtrack.

Xpressions

Going bald,
says Tulin.
Surely not?
You're too young.
What's caused the thinning?

Five heads face five mirrors, confess
the over application of Sun Blond,
that last, disastrous home perm.
One admits her lover *Likes to do*
strange things with a hairbrush,
another *That she can still feel*
the plaits her mother wove.

Here's sanctuary
to relieve a frazzled mop,
the choke of too much hairspray.
Tea and a turn
through the pages of *STYLE* renew
the possibilities - Tulin's secret shampoo,
you can't buy it in Boots.
Serated edge scissors shape curls
that fight back in the kitchen,
confound the strongest wind machine.

Arriving mouse, you leave vixen,
Phyl waits by the basin to baptise us,
Minh sweeps up the long and shortfall,
Tina tempers the heat of the dryer.

All you need's good gossip
and the deep knowledge gleaned
from each follicle, or a wig,
they can do those too.

Before we leave the salon
Tulin tests the cut,
ensures the sides are more even.

Break

Once a day, the Poor Claires congregate
round a snooker table instead of the altar,
practice their skills with the cue,
time off from saving souls,
denying the devil.

But the nuns play every shot
with the same vigilance and devotion
they bring to prayer,
faith marvellous to contemplate,

difficult to anchor in the round -
less black and white,
the red, green, blue, brown,
pink and yellow balls
connect the shots.
Reputation has it their aim
is little short of miraculous.

I'd need to see it in the flesh;
the best of my belief is keeping
one or two balls back
in case there's any doubt
but I can see how renouncing
worldly attachments would hone the focus,

other proofs pending.

Finishing Line

Body hostage to a perpetual course,
my ovaries like small, faithful
magicians' hats popping eggs,

left or right, I could feel it,
then the roll through the fallopian tube
like a rite of passage
to the womb's holding space,
rich in oxygen, nutrients.
The doctor said, *You could drown
in that blood and survive.*

But we call it a curse,
month after month,
an urge to throw knives
and mean to,
that pelvic ache
as though some force
is pulling me down to the centre,
no means to resist.

Thirteen when I started,
two pregnancies,
four hundred and forty four periods,
a flawless circuit
but since the last, nothing -
weeks now.

Longest of marathons,
expelling and replenishing
a hundreweight of blood.

Close up,
you can smell the iron.

Cleavage

Cup size is heading for Z,
the rise and rise of silicone,

paradise for a bold climber
if you can slip a hand in,

get a grip,
latch mouth to summit.

The higher you go,
the thinner the air

around the nipple.

Dimensions

The first time I saw an erect penis in the flesh
I ran away: that the thing could grow
so big and stiff
and urgent. He said *Feel it.*
I fled.

Later, I felt my way round my vagina,
such a small opening.
I couldn't imagine how it could accommodate
anything longer or larger than a finger.
I thought God must have got the size of the parts
wrong, considered celibacy.

It takes time to grasp the dimensions
of penis and vagina
and even now the measurements puzzle me -
their stretch and reach,
then again, sometimes,
how tight the fit.

Inheritance

From my mother, proof
that life is too difficult.

From my father, proof
that life holds on.

From them both, a daughter
torn, believing one, without

denying the other.

Near Death (Domestic)

The washing machine,
worn out with the effort
of keeping things clean,
flooded.

Marooned on the diminishing carpet,
like trippers watching the tide come in,
he yelled *Swim for the insurance policy.*

They rescued what they could,
the kids, cat, spoons,
mopped up,
everything but the stains –
bruises on the shag pile,
high tide marks on the walls,
the anaglypta flowers drowned.

She's for getting out,
cancelling all claims,
but the damp's got into the door frames
and the new carpet already laid,
cut, stretched to fit the corners.

They've made it home again.

Windolene

Soft and pink.
Soaks up the dirt a treat
mum said, rubbing hard.

During the divorce
she took down all the curtains
and plastered the windows with the stuff.
The house was a pink tomb.

It dried to a tough finish –
mum and dad going for each other
like scouring pads and hammers.

Me and my brother left holding
the shammy leather.

Lexicon
for Irene

When you asked
how I felt
about the past
all I could say
was *I'm okay.*
Are you okay?
You nodded

but I knew you needed a larger explanation
for the lexicon of suicide we inherited -
how, every day, we look up *mum*
and still find her under *dead by her own hand,*
an error on the part of the Collins dictionary
I'm sure,

easily done
with around forty words to a page,
one thousand three hundred and ninety seven
pages, plus introduction,
thirty five million words on the web version
when it's finished, so the fly leaf says
and thesaurus
but that's been no help either
these forty years.

Take my hand:
Okay is a triumph

considering.

Suspending Belief
for my dad

*i **Pink Elephant***

Right now,
all I can think of is the pink elephant
that kept us company
the day we went to Greenwich Park
and sat by the Observatory
looking out over London
as if it were our whole world
and it was in that moment.
You asked *Who invented time?*

Your doctor has just taken me on one side,
told me firmly, quietly, sympathetically,
pink elephants don't exist
that it was just a man dressed up
but what does he know?

I don't know who invented time
but I'm working hard on an answer,
the pink elephant standing by.

ii   ***Feather House***

When I was young, bad dreams
chased me into the feather house.
Safe, I felt and heard your belly laugh
of reassurance.

I don't remember the first feather falling,
second or third.
You were a rare bird,
made good every loss

but now they've all come tumbling
and my hands have grown small again
trying to gather them.

iii South to North

May the fifth, nineteen ninety nine,
the journey over from south to north,
weather closing,
colder than ever

but I got there in time
to hold your hand
and gently trace the line of veins,
like roots. Oak,

you gave life up, a feather.
Death didn't defeat us.
It's this afterwards
slogging through it

keeps taking me back
and with each anniversary
I set out again.

iv **Dancing**

And then I glimpsed you dancing,
dancing in heaven.
It looked like the pictures
they showed us at Sunday School.

Sunday School, remember –
I always kicked against the pew
and never was persuaded into the fold,
tugging hard at the fabric,
insisted God was no more real
than the pink elephant.
You had faith enough for both of us.

Only, just before you died, you cried
knowing we couldn't be reunited after death,
my disbelief put me one side of the gates,
you the other.

But in that moment
we reached through to touch again,

the pink elephant, smiling.

Love and the Law of My Children

Robert takes tea with no sugar
but coffee demands at least two spoonfuls.

I stand with the kettle poised, wonder
if this will be a tea or coffee day.

Louise drinks neither tea nor coffee,
prefers water, drawn from her own well.

I dip and dip again into her blue brown eyes,
my bucket barely skims the surface.

My Most Faithful Audience

You weren't there when I turned
seven, started secondary school,
had my first period,
walked up the aisle,
delivered your grandchildren,
went back to college and got a degree,
became a successful career woman,

wrote a poetry collection
and put the first signed copy
with all my love, carefully
under a Rosemary bush
I planted for you earlier today
to the sound of your familiar applause.
How your hands must ache by now.

Time for you
to leave the auditorium.

Touching the Grain
for Phil

Without a bed
and wondering why,
he went to the park to think about it -
a bench handy to help settle his thoughts.
It made no demands of him
beyond the moment.

Tired of thinking,
he slept –
let his dreams dust off the branches,
found that the bench
was as good as a bed

so he stayed
all summer and early autumn,
learned its contours,
leaned into it like a friend,

warm in advance of winter.

Soundings

The guide book insists Venice is sinking.
We are walking by a canal at night.
Beneath the surface
I can see the city's future,
its grandeur and dilapidation,
the Ponti di Sespiri breathing
its last on the lagoon bed,
the bells we heard ring out
in the Campanile di San Marco
rusted and silent,
the shimmer of a gondola adrift
without oarsman or lovers.

For you and I
still rising to each other,
Venice floats fragile, unfounded.
We turn the pages,
take soundings above
and below the water line.

Funny Bones

Always a comic,
quick fire, knockabout lines
and the audience like them.
Keep your readers laughing -
you don't get any more bouquets
for a tragedy. Back stage

too many vases stand empty
but not the way I write it,
you can turn anything round with humour,
even a child's heartbreak. Seven,
when I cracked my first joke, sharp edged
but it got their attention. They said
You are a funny bones.

Snap, snap, snap
but I'm still standing,
a lop sided clown,
nothing if not entertaining.

Final Soundtrack

Thinking about the songs I'd like played
at my funeral, all that occurs as apt
is *Nellie the Elephant*,
where she *Packs her trunk*
and says goodbye to the circus,
the Head of the Herd calling,
trundles off to the great elephant graveyard,
leaves a large and lovely footprint in the world,
one you could cradle a child in
and never turned rogue.

There's time yet,
some consolation and a large relief
to the rest of the big top,
the havoc I've caused
for a person with relatively small feet.
Trump, trump, trump.

RSVP

The invitation is welcome
but with me as a guest, you might
want to reconsider.

I get my feet too far under the table.
If there's a wobbly leg
I'll find it, bring a saw for a gift.

A long night ahead –
those sharp edged small hours
when the answers turn truthful.

The door again,
so soon?